Spiritual Zen
Paradigm Shift

DOUG PAMENTER

Author: Doug Pamenter
Editor: Brenda Nicell
Illustrator: Graeme Partridge-David

© SPIRITUAL ZEN LOGO

The Spiritual Zen logo is a visual gestalt that combines an outline of a dove and an open circle. The blue dove represents spirit. The green circle represents the unity and tranquility of Zen. The circle is open to suggest that life is an experiential journey. Together they depict the relationship we all have with ourselves, with others and with source, and it is in exploring the nature of these relationships that we achieve enlightenment.

The purposes of words
are to convey ideas.
When the ideas are grasped
the words are forgotten.
Chuang-Tzu

CONTENTS

CONTENTS

PREFACE

Look and see something new.
What you are seeing is the same.
Yet, why is your understanding different?

Spiritual Zen is the manifestation of a new paradigm. It is the expression of all that is currently happening in the world today in terms of spiritual exploration, quantum physics and religious practice. It embraces all beliefs, but speaks to a personal truth and a shared universal truth. You recognize it in your daily life when you are in flow with yourself, others and your surroundings—the world at large. It is all around you, it is in you and you are a part of it.

A connecting thread guides our way.
There are many currents in the river.

This book outlines the path by which millions of people are simultaneously walking. There are times when we may stumble or seem to lose our way. Yet, when we reach out with our spirit we no longer have to worry about the careful placement of each step. Even though the path is rarely completely clear, a part of us always knows that it is there before us just waiting to be discovered.

Which path am I to follow?
If only I could fly as a bird and see beyond.

You are reading this book because you were meant to. Whatever the circumstances that brought you to this moment—here you are. There may be something contained within the pages, just for you, or perhaps for you to relay to someone else. You may be seeking a deeper spiritual understanding of yourself, of what your purpose in life is, how to improve your meditative practice, or are simply curious about what Spiritual Zen might be. Welcome home.

CHAPTER 1: APPROACHING SPIRITUAL ZEN

Everyone Experiences Zen Moments

Not everyone has heard of Zen, but everyone has experienced it. Even though you may not have realized it in the moment that it was occurring. A Zen experience is uniquely unique. For some people Zen is appreciating a deeper understanding of them self, and for others it is a flood of peace and joy. No two Zen experiences are alike. Zen hates repetition. Zen is moving beyond from looking inside.

You cannot hear an experience.
Who has not heard of Zen?

Everyone has Experienced Spiritual Zen

Spiritual Zen is Zen turned inside out and stretched to infinity. It is a natural extension of Zen Buddhism or simply Zen, into the realm of universal vibrational energy flow, or the source energy of the universe. It engulfs both science and religion, yet embraces neither. The eclectic term Spiritual Zen has been coined to describe a state of shared enlightenment that assimilates the latest advances in global scientific understanding as well as each individual's spiritual beliefs. Spiritual Zen is expansive yet uniquely personal.

In Spiritual Zen, the concept of *quantum entanglement* is embraced, such that our spiritual energy gets co-mingled or entangled with all those persons with whom we have had conscious thought or physical contact with in our lives. An example might be when you are thinking about a particular person with whom you have a strong connection, there is a strong possibility that they are thinking of you too. Vibrational energy always flows. Through our thoughts and feelings we can connect with vibrational energy or block it. Negative emotions like shame and guilt may coincide with low vibrational forms of energy and the person may feel emotionally stuck. Thoughts and emotions, like love and gratitude, are believed by many to have a higher frequency.

1

These higher forms of energy produce a lighter transcendent feeling and perhaps even a sense of flow and deep spiritual connection.

> *"All matter originates and exists only by virtue of a force which brings the particle of an atom to vibration and holds this most minute solar system of the atom together. We must assume behind this force the existence of a conscious and intelligent mind. This mind is the matrix of all matter."* Max Planck

Spiritual Zen is the fruit of the tree produced by grafting universal spirituality to modern Zen. It is realizing our outward unseen connection to others as well as our inner connection to our deepest self. Spiritual Zen is a blurring of individual and collective experiences in a way that challenges definable boundaries. Even the term Spiritual Zen is a bit of an enigma as it brings together two seemingly divergent terms. This author proposes that the blending of universal spirituality and Zen mindfulness is the transcendent connection we are all seeking.

Spiritual Zen suggests that *"spirit energy"* or *"source"* is the sum of the energy fields of the universe and is of intelligent design. It is the creative flow of spiritual energy or *"intelligent source,"* which brought forth the various particles, which form the mass of the universe and allows corporeal life to flourish. We are the product of intelligent source.

The universe itself is an expanding field of energy field. Matter is created by the interaction of the various energy fields within it. The evidence is clear that there is more to the universe than simple Newtonian physics. Einstein explained the relationship between energy and mass with his famous $E=MC^2$ equation. The Standard Model of quantum physics predicted the existence of the Higgs Boson or *"God Particle,"* and it was later discovered using the Large Hadron Collider at CERN with a mass of 125 GeV. What was once only theoretical has been proven. Currently scientists are looking for evidence of the existence of additional particles in the 2 TeV range. Our learning expands along with the universe.

What exactly is the *"source energy"* of the universe? The answer is that no one truly knows, but modern quantum physicists have lots of theories and experimental physicists are doing their best to create experiments to learn as much as they can. The basic understanding is that empty space is not empty. Just because we cannot see something does not mean that there is nothing there. Consider the force that a magnet projects and you will get the idea.

2

Is the fish aware of the water it is swimming in?
Are humans aware of the spiritual flow
of energy around them?

Do you believe that the universe is of intelligent design and that there is a force that holds it all together? If you do, then how shall we strive to interact with this force or source energy? Spiritual Zen suggests that we are made of stardust and through our choices we can choose to flow with and be a part of the dynamic intelligence of the universe. We participate daily through our thoughts, feelings, and actions as we create our lives and interact with the energy flow of others.

Learning to Flow

The ultimate goal of Spiritual Zen is to experience a sense of being attuned to the dynamic flow of life. To be fully immersed in this flow.
Metaphorically, much like flowing with the current in a vast ever-changing river. It is being immersed in what you are doing, whom you are with and what you are focused on. It is realizing that there is *intelligent design* in the universal flow of energy, thought, space and time and *you* are a part of it.

Historical Zen

To approach an understanding of Spiritual Zen, one must have at least a rudimentary understanding of the evolution of Zen. Thus, both will be compared and contrasted throughout this book.

Zen is more of a philosophy than a religion, but could also be considered a movement—a way of approaching satori *(enlightenment)*. Two instrumental teachers of Zen Buddhism who taught in the West, were Daisetz Teitaro Suzuki and Shunryu Suzuki. Their focus and practice vary somewhat, but their core tenets are the same.

According to David Schiller in the **LITTLE ZEN COMPANION,** *"Zen began in China in the sixth century as a meeting of Indian Buddhism with Taoism, merging the speculative with the practical, the metaphysical with the earthy. Zen arrived in Japan about 1190, where the houses of Soto and Rinzai continue to flourish. The first Zen teachers came to America around 1905."*

Daisetz Teitaro Suzuki taught classes at Columbia University in the 1950s and helped usher Zen into mainstream North America. His seminal book **AN INTRODUCTION TO ZEN BUDDHISM** was based upon original manuscripts from 1914 and 1927, and was first published in 1964. He depicted *"Zen in its essence as the art of seeing into the nature of one's being and it points the way from bondage to freedom."*

To Daisetz, the attainment of satori is the raison d'être *(reason for existence)* of Zen. Satori is both an art and a way of approaching an enlightened state of being.
Satori or sudden enlightenment comes as something unexpected that cannot be willed into existence.

A number of years later on the west coast of America, Shunryu Suzuki's talks following Zazen meditation were recorded and formulated into the **ZEN MIND, BEGINNERS MIND** book, published in 1970. Shunryu stressed: right practice, right attitude, and right understanding. It is this Soto Way that has come to be synonymous with Zen as it is commonly practiced today. Robert M. Pirsig elucidated this approach in his book **ZEN AND THE ART OF MOTORCYCLE MAINTENANCE.**

> *"So, the thing to do when working on a motorcycle, as in any other task, is to cultivate the peace of mind, which does not separate one's self from one's surroundings. When this is done successfully, then everything else follows naturally. Peace of mind produces right values, right values produce right actions, and right actions produce work which will be a material reflection for others to see the serenity at the center of it all."*

Where is God in Traditional Zen?

Zen Buddhism does not recognize a separate personhood of God whose depths are to be fathomed. Zen is a bottomless abyss. This is consistent with the Buddhist doctrine of emptiness. In Zen, God is neither denied nor insisted upon. *The spiritual essence of God is everywhere.*

The focus of Zen is on the *spiritual nature of a person expressed through their experiences.* **Only personal experiences are truly real due to their tangible nature.** Yet to achieve enlightenment a person must transcend their experiences. A Zen perspective acknowledges that in every person there is inner purity and goodness. A fundamental objective of Zen is to meditate upon the real nature of one's own mind or soul. The discipline of Zen consists in opening the mental third eye in order to look into the very reason of existence.

> *What do you know, if not from your experience?*
> *What can you prove, except that there is more to learn?*

Zen teaching talks about our Buddha nature, which is often equated with the satori experience. One description said it is freeing you from the cycle of birth and death. *"It is to die completely and come back to life."* The only apparent way to escape from the endless cycle of reincarnation is to achieve satori or Buddha nature.

> *What face did you wear before you were born?*
> *Uncover yourself and see eternity.*

Christians talk about being *"born again"* in the spirit. Could these two different points of view be talking about the same thing albeit from a different cultural and historical perspective? Are the doctrines so rigid as to deny any possible similarities? Are we humans really so different?

Unity and Degrees of Separation

One of the core truths of Zen is that *all is one – unity.* That is why a circle is representative of Zen. When drawn, the opening at the bottom of the Zen circle suggests that we do not have all the answers. A pure Zen approach does not acknowledge any form of dualism such as the Taoist or Daoist view of *(Yin and Yang).* While it may be useful to examine behaviors or situations using terms such as good and evil, it is the integration of both perspectives, which tends to bring forth lasting resolution.

Similarly, in Spiritual Zen, the approach is to consider both the relative terms of good and evil as part of the whole. How can a good God create evil? If the answer is our ability to exercise **free will**, then it makes sense that **our choices and actions** can draw us closer to each other or further apart. Can we alter the state of our soul *(the vibrational frequency of our spiritual essence)* through the various choices we make in life?

Spiritual Zen explores the notion that there is a malleable degree of connection to source energy or separation from source energy. A heaven experience would generally be considered as quite connected. In the Christian Bible **2 Corinthians 12:2** it is written: *"I know a man in Christ who fourteen years ago was caught up to the third heaven. Whether it was in the body or out of the body I do not know—God knows."* So, apparently even in heaven there is a degree of stratification.

From a Spiritual Zen perspective, **we all have a core spirit with a changeable vibration based on our thoughts, emotions, actions and life pattern**. Raising our vibration through mindful-flow, prayer or meditation helps us to connect to our own spiritual essence and that of others. Upon our eventual physical death, our spiritual essence naturally becomes a part of the frequency of the energy field of the universe that it matches. Souls with higher vibrations being more connected to source, lower vibrations less connected.

Cross the bridge and you do not arrive.
Stay as you are and you will never get there.

Zen Makes No Claims

Zen differs from all other philosophic and religious meditation practices in its principle lack of supposition. Zen makes no claims for spiritual truth. A person who practices Zen meditation is encouraged to seek out his or her own truth, his or her own path to enlightenment.

One day, a stranger approached the Zen Master and pressured him to expound on his views, he replied: *"I really have nothing to impart to you, and if I tried to do so, you might make me an object of ridicule."*

In a similar manner, Spiritual Zen does not believe that it is any better or worse than any other approach to spirituality. It merely encourages the contemplation of the vibrational energy of the universe as the medium in which we flow, just as the fish swims in water. With Spiritual Zen, like Zen, it is the experience that has significance, not any number of conceptual examples, so that no one person's truth is ever pushed on another.

> ***What is the energy field that fills the universe?***
> ***Ask a fish about the water it swims in.***

Significance and Actualization of Zen

One day, a monk approached the master who was working in the garden. He asked the master, how to find the deepest meaning in Zen. The master sat down on a bench and motioned for the monk to sit as well. The monk was somewhat confused at the silence that followed. After sitting for a while, he asked the master to show him how to use Zen in every day life. The master stood up and continued to work in the garden.

> ***Form your hands into a bowl and you can drink.***
> ***Grasp the water and you will remain thirsty.***

Afterlife

Does anyone truly know what happens to our soul when we die? What if our soul or spiritual essence when freed from our physical body becomes expansive and transcendent? What if our spiritual essence just disintegrates into the background energy of the universe?

Zen neither asserts nor denies the existence of an afterlife; it merely suggests that there is unity in enlightenment. Spiritual Zen affirms a belief in an afterlife where our spiritual essence continues when our physical body has died. However, who knows what the state or nature of our transcendent spiritual essence will be. One possible notion is that each person's spiritual essence fits in with similar vibrational energy frequencies and flows with the spiritual energy of the universe.

In the book **PROOF OF HEAVEN**, Dr. Eben Alexander explained how he was a Harvard trained neurosurgeon of 25 years who he fell into a coma for seven days due to severe bacterial meningitis. During this time, his consciousness disengaged from his body and he had what he described as a journey into the afterlife experiencing both heavenly and not so heavenly realms.

Before his experience he did not believe in the existence of a non-physical spirit. However, after returning to his body and experiencing a miraculous healing he stated that the afterlife seem more real than his earthly existence, all communication was telepathic and the fabric of the afterlife was pure love.

When the mind is enlightened, the spirit is free, and the body matters not.

CHAPTER 2: THE PURPOSE OF SPIRITUAL ZEN

The Emergence of a New Paradigm

Spiritual Zen is the confluence of 21st century spirituality and Zen as it is generally practiced in the Western world. It embodies our deepest relationship with and knowledge of ourselves, our relationships and spiritual connectedness to others, and is expressed each day as we flow with the source energy of the universe. It is a paradigm that is shared and practiced by many, but recognized by few—until now. Perhaps you already are a part of the Spiritual Zen movement and have been following your own core truths for years even though your experience has not yet been labeled. The common tenets include:

- The recognition of personal transformative and transcendent experiences.
- The belief in the universal energy field or source energy of the universe.
- The practice of mindfulness as expressed in meditation or prayer as a means of spiritually connecting with self, with others, and with source *(all living things)*.

Spiritual Zen speaks to a core personal truth within each of us and a shared universal truth as a reflection of our human experience. Our **personal truth** is relative to our experiences in life, our level of knowledge, and our emotional interpretation of our life events. When we are in tune with another person, quite often our personal truth fits with their personal truth. Eventually this process leads to a **universal truth**, which is shared by many. Once your perspective has expanded to embrace universal spirituality, you have achieved a paradigm shift and are awakening to Spiritual Zen.

> *Sleep with a question. Wake with an answer.*
> *The body dies, the spirit rises.*

Living out Your Purpose

Who has not thought about or wondered what their life purpose is? Should we seek to discover our life purpose or is it up to us as individuals to create our life purpose? From a Spiritual Zen perspective, our life purpose continually evolves as we experience life in communion with others and source.

Some people have a sense that there is a unique purpose or destiny to be fulfilled in their life and others believe that we also have a collective destiny or purpose with those who share in our lives. A Spiritual Zen connection is realized when you appreciate divine appointments as more than mere coincidences.

Words like synchronicity and law of attraction become more than mere ideas, but a way of life. People are transcending daily suffering and experiencing moments of enlightenment, vibrational energy flow and universal abundance.

Enlightenment sinks to the soul and meets eternity.

Spiritual Zen strives to engender a wordless heartfelt truth, not to communicate an idea. In other words, our purpose is to deeply and pervasively experience a God of our understanding in all that we think, feel and do. This challenge was well described by Erich Fromm:

"We try to evade the question [of existence] with property, prestige, power, production, fun, and ultimately, by trying to forget that we—that I—exist. No matter how often he thinks of God or goes to church, or how much he believes in religious idea, if he, the whole man, is deaf to the question of existence, if he does not have an answer to it, he is marking time, and he lives and dies like one of the million things he produces. He thinks of God, instead of experiencing God."

"I am the source of all material and spiritual worlds.
Everything emanates from me." Bhagavad-Gita

A Shared Journey

Our purpose is to experience the deepest possible relationship with our self, with others and with source. A Spiritual Zen perspective is simplicity of life, service to others, and life-long learning. Everyone's individual journey is uniquely their own and at the same time we are a part of a large community. We each have this beautiful gift that we can share with others. In a sense we are born with pieces to each other's puzzle and we need to interact with each other to complete them.

How sad when a gift offered is not received.
How sad when a gift is withheld that is needed.

Similarly our core spirit leads us to choose the experiences of our lives. One person might choose to travel a lot and maximize their external experiences. Another person might choose to spend a great deal of time in quiet meditation, looking inward for a deeper experience. It is an individual life and an individual spirit, and at the same time, a cosmic life and a cosmic spirit.

Zen meditation uses real experiences as a means to open the mind of the person meditating to achieve moments of enlightenment and embrace an insight into the nature of self. The experience is emancipation from a conscious form of illusionary conception of self. In other words, the experience of meditation frees us from how we see ourselves and what we believe about ourselves based on how others see us. An example is a picture does not accurately depict who you are. A video of your whole life might provide more information but still does not accurately represent all of who you are. You are so much more than any illusionary conception of yourself. Likewise we are so much more than other people's perceptions of us.

Spiritual Zen extends this raison d'être to a level of relationship, of having a deep connection with self, with others, and with something greater than yourself and others. A Spiritual Zen experience is a sense of being *"one with,"* the vibrational flow that surrounds all of us, rather than a momentary awareness of an experience beyond the banal familiar. The greatest truth of the universe—is unity!

Abundance is not Poverty

Spiritual Zen recognizes the materialistic world in which we live and advocates a life of gratitude and generosity towards others. Spiritual Zen is similar to traditional Zen whose goal is to make the best use of all items and not wasting anything. Yet, the Spiritual Zen goal is to obtain what we need and not always what we want. When we are blessed with an abundance of time, treasure and talent it allows for generosity towards others.

Stewardship is sharing with others the gifts
of one's life, time, talents, and resources
without expecting anything in return.

Spiritual Zen flows with Source

Spiritual Zen accepts that there is a connecting force that extends throughout the entire universe and that this vibrational flow of energy has an intelligent purposeful design. The practice of Spiritual Zen is to mindfully attune our spiritual essence with this source energy as much as possible. A Christian might describe this as aligning the individual's will with the will of God.

Spiritual Zen does not affirm the supposition that we are Buddha or God, in the largest possible understanding. We may come from "source," have "source" within us, and return to "source," but we are NOT "source." A Spiritual Zen paradigm suggests that source energy or God is that which connects all that is in the universe.

A drop of water is not the ocean.
When it rains, the drops can be seen.
When the rivers flow and return to the ocean,
who knows if the drops are distinguishable or not?

An interesting historical footnote is that Zen was sometimes called *"the way,"* just as was the early Christian church and Taoism. Is there a common truth rooted in these different religious approaches? Are there similar spiritual—thinking, feeling, and acting life-paths that speak to each of our individual hearts?

Only what grows out of yourself is your own knowledge,
everything else is borrowed plumage.

Is there a Physiological Explanation for Spirituality?

Scientists have described *N,N-dimethyltryptamine* or DMT as the *"Spirit Molecule,"* which is in or can be created within all living organisms, both plants and animals. It has been described as the language of plants—the messenger molecule by which plants use to mediate their relationships with other organisms in their environment.

It is believed that when humans experience spiritual phenomena it may be due in part to an endogenous *(from within)* release of DMT in the pineal glands of our brains. While the release of DMT seems to instigate the spiritual experience, the experience itself is not confined to a physiological reaction between the brain and body, but is often described as an out-of-body or spiritually expanding journey.

The practice of prayer, meditation or simply being in an environment conducive to a mindful-state may facilitate the release of this natural chemical in our brains and engender a sense of flow and connection. When we practice *"quiet listening" (prayer, meditation)* it expands our perspective to include others, the environment and spiritual matters. When we teach our children to listen quietly, it helps instill in them a sense of who they are and how everything in the universe is connected.

The **pineal gland** has been described as our **third eye** going back to the time of the ancient Egyptians and perhaps even further to the time of the Sumerians and other pre-history human eras. Today there are First Nations societies in South American who use Ayahuasca a DMT tea made from the combination of two natural ingredients to help participants connect to the deeper part of themselves and to experience something beyond themselves.

Researchers using exogenous *(created outside the body)* DMT on human volunteers were led to the belief that *"disembodied consciousness is a possibility."* One researcher even went so far as to described DMT as the common molecular language among all living beings on this planet and maybe even other planets.

What is enlightenment,
but awakening to the eternal in the here and now.

What is Spirituality to you?

Spiritual Zen is only truly spiritual in the sense that you are challenged to figure out what being connected spiritually to self, others, and source means to you. Does it make a difference if you substitute the words *"vibrational energy"* for spirituality?

> *"The letter must never be followed, only the spirit is to be grasped. Higher affirmations live in the spirit. And where is the spirit? Seek it in your everyday experience, and therein lies abundance of proof for all you need."* Diasetz Tietaro Suzuki

Your task, as you read through this book and work through the exercises, is to approach your own understanding of the experience of Spiritual Zen. Keep in mind, that your perception of the experience is not the experience, just as *the finger pointing at the moon is not the moon*.

CHAPTER 3: THE PRACTICE OF SPIRITUAL ZEN

What Makes Zen – Zen?

Two significant features of Zen are the use of Koan anecdotes and Zazen meditation. Koan literally means a public document or authoritative statute. It now denotes some anecdote of an ancient master, a dialogue between master and monks, or a statement put forward by a teacher, all of which are used as the means for opening one's mind to the truth of Zen.

At the heart of Zen practice is Zazen, or sitting in absorption. The aim of Zazen meditation is first to still the mind, then through years of practice, to reach a state of pure, thought-free wakefulness so that the mind can realize its own Buddha-nature. Zazen is itself enlightenment.

Today people may use the term Zen when they believe an object or experience to be calm, uncluttered, or patterned without exact duplication. People have created *"Zen gardens"* to help visitors achieve a mindful state. However, the experience of Zen is so much more than a visit to a Zen garden, just as a picture of you can hardly be compared to the experience of meeting you in person and having a face-to-face conversation.

A Zen experience deliberately defies all concept making. Zen perceives or feels and does not abstract nor mediate. Zen penetrates and is finally lost in the immersion. Zen and Spiritual Zen both defy convenient labels. To label the experience is to lose the perception of the experience.

> *Look into yourself, and see others looking out at you.*
> *Gaze through their eyes, and see forever.*

Zen strives to come in contact with the inner workings of our being, and to do that in the most direct manner possible. Similarly, Spiritual Zen strives to come in contact with the nature of our relationship to self, to others and to something that encompasses self and others.

In the famous *"flower sermon"* of Buddha. He held up a flower to a gathering of monks, without uttering a word. Apparently only one monk understood him.

Silent the flower talks. Ears that hear are tingled.

According to Eckhart Tolle in **A NEW EARTH – AWAKENING TO YOUR LIFE'S PURPOSE**, *"Seeing beauty in a flower could awaken humans, however briefly, to the beauty that is an essential part of their own innermost being, their true nature. This first recognition of beauty was one of the most significant events in the evolution of human consciousness."*

Monastery Life

In the words of Diasetz Teitaro Suzuki, the meditation hall or Zendo was where the Zen master educated its' monks. To understand how it was regulated, is to get a historical glimpse into the practical and disciplinary aspects of Zen Buddhist life.

Each monk was allotted one tatami, or a mat 3 feet by 6 feet, where he sat, meditated and slept. The monk's bedding never exceeded one quilt 5 feet by 6 feet.

The monks guiding principle was: *A day of no work is a day of no eating*. The monk's body was kept busy to keep their mind busy, fresh, wholesome and alert. Conviction was gained through experience and not through abstraction. No work was considered to be beneath their dignity, and a perfect feeling of brotherhood prevailed among them. The industry of the monks was proverbial. To say that something was like a Zen temple, meant that the place was in the neatest possible order.

Asceticism, which is the doctrine that a person can attain a high spiritual and moral state by practicing self-denial and self-mortification, was not the ideal of life for Zen monks; nor was any other ethical system. *The central idea, of the monk's life was not to waste, but to make the best possible use of all things they received.* They put into action whatever reflections they made during hours of *"quiet sitting"* and thus tested their validity in the vital field of actualities.

The basic principle of the Zendo is learning by doing. The outward communal tasks of living and inner aspirations, working together upon the character of the monk, often end in producing a fine specimen of humanity called a full-fledged Zen master.

Zen theoretically encompasses the whole universe and is not bound by rules of antithesis. Maintaining humility is why the Zendo plays such a great part in historical Zen teaching. The reason the Zen monastery is so strict is that pride of heart may depart and the cup of humility be drunk to the dregs. The power of an illuminating Zen insight must go hand-in-hand with a deep sense of humility and meekness of heart.

Humility and Acceptance

Humility and acceptance are very important aspects of Zen and Spiritual Zen. Humility is a non-defensive spirit when confronted, having nothing to prove to others, nothing to defend with regard to your own actions, nothing to lose *(non-attachment, only gratitude)*, and an authentic desire to help others. Acceptance is embracing what ever comes your way as if you had chosen it. This is not a fatalistic attitude, but one of non-resistance, flowing with life.

There once was a Zen master Hakuin who was praised by his neighbors for living a pure life. In the village was a family with a beautiful daughter who owned a fish market. Suddenly, without any warning, her parents discovered she was with child. This made her parents angry. She would not confess who the man was but after much harassment, at last named Hakuin.

In great anger the parents went to the master. *"Is that so?"* was all he would say. After the child was born, it was brought to Hakuin to look after. By this time he had lost his reputation, which did not trouble him. He took very good care of the child. He obtained milk from his neighbors and everything else the child needed.

A year later the girl-mother could stand it no longer. She told her parents the truth - the real father of the child was a young man who worked in the fish market. The mother and father of the girl at once went to Hakuin to ask forgiveness, to apologize at length, and to get the child back. Hakuin was willing. In yielding the child, all he said was: *"Is that so?"*

What do I have that is not for service to others?

Where can I find Spiritual Zen?
Look within, it has always been there.

Practicing Spiritual Zen

The practice of Spiritual Zen is unique to each individual. Spiritual Zen meditation or prayer encourages the full engagement in whatever activity you are doing. It is mindful-awareness such that the individual has a sense of being immersed into the activity, a sense of connection with self and others if they are present—a state of clear focus and flow.

> ***Flow is being completely connected to all that is around you, while feeling totally unconstrained by thought, emotions or your physical body.***

For some people having a quiet place free of distractions to meditate or pray is important. For other people it is completely engaging in an activity to the point where every cell in their body feels fully alive. Some people feel most connected when they are surrounded by nature or even focused on a task. The important aspect of Spiritual Zen practice is that it is done regularly with intention and appreciation.

CHAPTER 4: THE PROCESS OF SPIRITUAL ZEN

A Spiritual Approach

Spiritual Zen is a way of approaching *oneness with the universe*. This can be done in as many different ways as there are people practicing Spiritual Zen. The key is to determine which practices work for you. **The focus is on the process,** without affirming any method in particular.

The process of Zen according to Shunryu Suzuki is: right practice, right attitude, and right understanding. With Spiritual Zen, the process is: *right thinking* [cognitions], *right feelings* [affect] and *right actions* [behaviors], and the three domains should be in a state of dynamic balance with each other.

A Secular Paradigm

Many forms of psychological treatments have been developed to re-balance these domains. For example, Cognitive Therapy *(thinking)*, Person-Centered Therapy *(feelings)*, and Behavioral Therapy *(actions)*, or a combination of two domains, such as Cognitive-Behavioral Therapy. There is no end to the variety of therapy styles, and many more are produced in support of the modern education system conveyor belt of PhD candidates. It is not surprising how easy it is to disconnect the individual from their true reality by the application of diagnostic labels.

> *Wake the person with their eyes wide open.*
> *Who has ears open, but hears not?*

The past is nothing more than a place where we have been. Accept the past without judgment. Re-connect with yourself, with others and with source. Live your best dream until it is all you remember. No label can ever accurately describe your true nature, your true self.

The deepest truths of Zen cannot be made the subject of logical exposition; they are to be experienced in the innermost soul. Zen most strongly and persistently insists on an inner spiritual experience.

Carl Jung described the Zen experience of satori saying: *"The answers will come to you from a void, the light which flares up from the black darkness, these have always been experiences of wonderful and blessed illumination."*

> ***Where the mind leads the body follows.***
> ***Purpose flows from the heart.***

Non-Attachment

For some people, their greatest struggle is letting go or an emptying oneself of images. That is why repeating prayers or a mantra is helpful to some. The focus of Spiritual Zen is to fully immerse oneself in the experience so that you feel saturated, connected to the experience and transformed by it as you transcend from the physical, mental and emotional to completeness and oneness.

> ***When we let go of the image of what we think we want,***
> ***we allow the universe to give us something better.***

Attachment is the greatest illusion. It is saying: *"I will be happy when..."* The illusion is that something can suffice someone, and it is this illusion that stands behind all suffering and blocks all progress, and is one of the most difficult to overcome.

> ***Does a fish try to grasp the water it swims through?***
> ***Neither can you carry the path you walk on.***

Personal Experience is Everything

Personal experience is everything in Zen. You cannot be born for someone else. You cannot die for someone else. You cannot learn for someone else. The Zen experience is an inner spiritual experience. Spiritual Zen is a saturation of gratitude without being attached to anything. It is a sincere appreciation of all that we have without any sense of entitlement.

Practical Spiritual Zen

Spiritual Zen is eminently practical and fun. It is reality based in the *"here and now."* It achieves its goal of *"oneness"* - of perceiving that you are connected to and a part of something greater than yourself. It is in these moments when you experience what today is called eudemonia flow.

Now, eudemonia is a Greek term that could loosely be translated as *"human flourishing."* This again is a bit of a conceit since the universe has been around much longer than the ancient Greeks and I am sure that humans flourished long before they came up with a term for it.

One morning, a monk approached the master and asked; *"Where shall I go today to experience Zen?"* The master responded, *"Go wherever your feet take you?"* The monk sat down and meditated on what the master had said. Thinking he was clever, he decided to ask the same question the next day, and if he got the same response he would reply, *"but what if I had no feet?"* The following morning the monk approached the master and again asked; *"Where shall I go today to experience Zen?"* *"Go in whatever direction the wind blows"* responded the master.
Feeling frustrated, the monk thought to him self but what if there was no wind? He then decided to ask the master a third time the following day. On the third day when the monk asked the same question the master replied; *"Do what is required of you today and you will experience Zen."* In that moment the monk achieved enlightenment.

Your Experience of Spiritual Zen

Try to remember an experience when you have gotten lost in whatever you were doing, when time seemed to stand still, and you felt a sense of completeness or connection with yourself or with someone or something else. In those brief moments you achieved Spiritual Zen – peace, love, and joy. Now who would not want to experience that flavor again?

One way of personalizing your experience of Spiritual Zen is to create your own koans. Examples of koans are scattered throughout this book. They are the little phrases set apart in bold text, which are used to help you to contemplate more than the words and experience a deeper truth – or satori *(enlightenment)*. In addition to contemplating or writing your own koans there are an infinite number of ways to engage yourself in mindfulness and flow, such as: prayer, meditation, spending time in nature, with animals, or a person who is significant to you.

When time stands still you will find Spiritual Zen.

Transcend the Tangible

In Spiritual Zen, like in Zen Buddhism, all images are set aside, both figuratively and literally. Nothing must be present except what is actually there—your immediate experience. What is present is your conscious experience plus your unconscious beliefs. It is like asking someone to *"think outside of the box"* when they do not even realize that their thinking is *"in a box."*

Satori illuminates the darkness. Grasp it and it is gone.

What this means is not focusing on any tangible image, thing, or statue, such as a cross/crucifix, painting, or a statue of Buddha. Don't worry; you can still practice Spiritual Zen and maintain your own religious views. For example, while a cross may be symbolic of a person's relationship with Jesus Christ - the cross is not the relationship.

One of the key features of Spiritual Zen could be described as attentiveness, mindfulness or simply awareness. Attentiveness is, however, an effort of which we are not permanently capable. The Zen Buddhist strategy is to empty the conscious mind as much as possible of its contents. Then the energy of the conscious is transferred to the unconscious facilitating dreams or transformative bridging experiences. Spiritual Zen is slightly different; the focus is not on the mind being empty, but rather being immersed in the experience to the point where it becomes a transcendent moment.

Light always shines into darkness.
The smallest candle can light a whole room.
Uncover your light, and see for yourself.

Describing your Journey

Perhaps you would like to pause your reading and ponder your own Spiritual Zen experiences.

- Can you recall a time when you had a Spiritual Zen moment? What was it like?
- What does enlightenment means to you?
- What five words would you use to describe enlightenment? How about three words? Now, only one word.

_____

_____

_____

_____

_____

_____

_____

_____

_____

_____

CHAPTER 5: WHAT ARE ZEN KOANS?

The Journey is the Destination

Spiritual Zen is also a journey to self-discovery through the transformative process of conscious awareness or mindfulness. The challenge of *"experiencing beyond"* is one of the most difficult. Mostly because we refuse to give up or let go of our illusions of how we perceive reality. The conscious is only a part of the spiritual, and is never therefore capable of spiritual completeness. Zen demands intelligence and willpower to become real. If *the journey is the destination*, how will you know when you have arrived?

> **Master: *"Are you ready to begin?"***
> **Student: *"How will I know if I am ready?"***
> **Master: *"You are not ready."***

A monk once went to the Master and asked where the entrance to the path of truth was. The Master asked him: *"Do you hear the murmuring of the brook?" "Yes, I hear it,"* answered the Monk. *"There is the entrance,"* the Master instructed him.

The deepest truths of Zen cannot be made the subject of logical exposition; they arc to be experienced in the innermost soul. As a method of pure teaching Zen anecdotes (*koans*) are preferable to explanations. In using a koan, the Master chooses to *"speak less, but say more."*

A koan can be a paradoxical question, an expression or an action of the master. A good koan is neither a riddle nor a witty remark. It has a most definite objective, the arousing of doubt and pushing it to its furthest limits.

Traditional Zen koans are a paradox to be meditated upon as a way of training Zen Buddhist monks to abandon ultimate dependence on reason and to force them into gaining **sudden intuitive enlightenment**. In a similar manner, Spiritual Zen utilizes koans to facilitate self-awakened moments.

The difference in approaches is that if you undertake to do the exercises in this book—you must create your own koans. Thus, you become both the master and monk or teacher and student.

We teach best, what we most need to learn.
What do you not know?

You cannot be taught by another about yourself.

Zen exercises and Koans contain challenges that include:

- Freeing us from the misconception of self.
- Awakening our innermost wisdom - divine light, the source of: influence, power, kindness, justice, sympathy, impartial love, humanity, and mercy.
- Realizing we are identical in: spirit, essence, nature, and universal life.
- Opening ourselves to abundant grace, which arouses our moral nature, activates our spiritual eyes, and fills us with a sense of new capacity.

Zen is always New

Koans are of such great variety, such ambiguity and of such overwhelming paradox. Seldom is there a rational connection between the koan and the experience. Zen koans are to be experienced in the soul when they become for the first time intelligible. Personal experience, therefore, is everything in Zen.

The Zen method of training is practical and systematic. Zen is not a system founded upon the logic and analysis. Zen is the whole mind. Zen teaches nothing. We teach ourselves; Zen merely points the way.

Spiritual Zen is transformation to enlightenment through dynamically experiencing your own connection to the universe. Spiritual Zen also utilizes koans as a method of assisting the reader to contemplate ideas that extend the meaning of the words used. Whereas a Zen koan is used to facilitate a mental experience, a Spiritual Zen koan is used to facilitate the contemplation of a mental relationship as a life metaphor.

An Invitation to Participate

You are cordially invited to have fun and create your own koans to go with the topic guideposts in the following chapters. This can be done either on paper, or simply in your mind as you read through this book. After all, how you experience Spiritual Zen is up to you.

Your koans can be something that is personally meaningful to you or perhaps may enlighten others to a deeper experience. The basic guideline is that a koan may be: a **paradoxical question**, an **expression** or an **action**—with the objective of facilitating a spiritually connecting experience.

CHAPTER 6: CAN YOU KOAN?

Creating your own Spiritual Zen Koans

Throughout this book from the preface page to the epilogue there are many statements that are in bold, italics and centered. These statements are koans, which have been written by the author or where designated by other persons. The general goal of koans is to inspire the person reading it to seek out a deeper spiritual meaning beyond the actual words. An example is:

What is it that has spiritual meaning for you?
You will not find it in these words.

Can you think of a better way for you to experience Spiritual Zen than to create your own spiritually meaningful koans? Every person's life experiences are different, yet when we create a koan that another person is able to connect with or it resonates with them—we have achieved a level of shared Spiritual Zen enlightenment. Thus, I would like to encourage you to try to create your own koans whenever you see the double lines that go with the topics below.

Please also realize that there are as many ways of experiencing flow *(Spiritual Zen)*, as there are people. The illustrator experienced his own version of spiritual flow while creating the images you see throughout the book. When I appreciate the images he produced, I also experience a connecting flow. Similarly a dancer experiences spiritual flow through dynamic movement and when others are watching they empathically connect with the dancers emotional intentions. Who does not experience a sense of flow when participating in or watching a team sport?

Ride the Spiritual Wave

One-way of approaching Spiritual Zen is with the intent to ride the spiritual wave of connection to self, others, and source energy. What is it in your life that you naturally connect with? Keep in mind that the experience is not spiritual energy; it is merely a way of achieving the flow of spiritual energy in your life. Is a fish mindful of the water it is swimming in?

> ***Enlightenment cannot be experienced***
> ***in muddy waters.***

Awareness. Attentiveness. Mindfulness. How do you approach satori? *(Create your own koan.)*

_____

_____

My Personal Cause

Many people spend their whole lives trying to save other people, endangered animals, or the environment. Who or what are you trying to save? *(Create your own koan.)*

_____

_____

I saved you, but lost myself.
Now I save no one and all are saved.

Attitude is Everything

One day a student who was very judgmental of others approached her instructor with a complaint. The instructor acknowledged the student's feelings and explained to the student why the lesson was taught in such a manner. Not satisfied the student went away angry. A week later the student returned and asked the teacher *"if all was OK?"* The teacher who had appreciated the peace that ensued with the student's absence—stated that *"nothing had changed"* and was enlightened.

What can you teach me today?
Said the student to the teacher.

What can I learn from you?
Said the teacher to the student.

What is your attitude towards learning? *(Create your own koan.)*

_____

_____

If you give someone the answer,
they will not learn the lesson.

Holding onto the Past

You cannot pick up something new, until you let go of what is already in your hand. It takes effort to let go of past memories and feelings that are not edifying us. Are you still acting in the present based on your past experiences? Hurts, fears, insecurity? *(Create your own koan.)*

_____

_____

Look into your own hand and see what is there.
Now, throw it down.

Leaves fall from the tree once a year,
but it still grows strong and proud.

The Hunt for Self-Knowledge

There is no end to self-help books, and books about how to live your life correctly. Aristotle's famous saying, *"Know Thyself,"* is often repeated. However, there is a big difference between striving to know yourself as much as you can, and accepting yourself for who you are.

The path to self never ends.
Why are you still looking for it?

What are you trying to reveal about yourself? *(Create your own koan.)*

_____

_____

Kindness towards Others

Spiritual Zen encourages humility and acts of kindness towards others, without any thought of recompense or self-glorification. Karma is not a consideration in Spiritual Zen. Acting in love is within us.

A man always gave to the poor.
One day a TV crew recorded his actions.

When others saw his good works, he said:
"What has been seen is of no value."

Under what circumstances will you extend a kindness to others? *(Create your own koan.)*

_____

_____

Being True to Yourself

The person we deceive the most is always our self. This does not mean actual lies, but more often lies of self-deception, self-deprecation, and not believing in our full potential. When we are faced with the flow of love around us, our deepest feelings about ourselves often come to the surface.

The river tells no lies,
though standing on the shore,
the dishonest person hears them all.

When there is no sound but the river of love, what do you hear? *(Create your own koan.)*

_____

_____

The Volume of Silence

When silence and eloquence becomes identical, and where negation and assertion are unified - there is Spiritual Zen. Have you ever considered how *"loud"* the sound of silence really is?

Many years ago I had the opportunity to go cave exploring. After crawling deep into the cave all the noise of the outside world was silenced. I then became aware of a loud thumping and the sound of rushing fluid. I slowly realized that what I was hearing was the sound of blood flowing throughout my head and suddenly was enlightened to the volume of sound in my own body.

Music is the silence between the notes.

What do you hear in the silence? *(Create your own koan.)*

_____

_____

If the instrument is broken, the music will be sour.
The music does not play the musician.

What is the sound of your instrument? *(Create your own koan.)*

_____

_____

How do you connect with Nature? (flora and fauna)

What does being in nature do for you? *(Create your own koan.)*

_____

_____

Does a dog have a Buddhist nature?
Answer: **Wu** *(woof)*

Seasonal Spiritual Flow (Spring, Summer, Fall, Winter)

Many people have a powerful connection to the various seasons and man-made holidays throughout the year. Are there any particular seasons or holidays where you feel most connected? What about seasons or holidays that you might find particularly distressing? What other ways do you connect with the flow life beyond yourself?

(Create your own koan.)

_____

_____

Distractions

Spiritual Zen encourages separation from distractions. This includes all negative emotions such as resentments that inhibit the positive flow of spirit. The highest truth is an affirmation. To be free, life must be an absolute affirmation. It must transcend all possible conditions and limitations that hinder its free activity. In Spiritual Zen, facts are facts, and words are words. Each time Spiritual Zen is asserted things are vitalized; there is an act of creation.

Free your mind from distraction
and your actions will flow from your spirit.

Do not let an opportunity pass you by,
but think twice before acting.

Is there anything distracting you from acting with intention? *(Create your own koan.)*

_____

_____

Giving Generously

Consider all the good that you have in your life. We all have: **Time, Treasure, and Talents** that we can share with others. Yet, what keeps us from sharing more freely? Is it because we have *"earned"* what we have? We *"worked hard"* and *"deserve"* to reap the fruits of our labor! What about those persons who have not had the same opportunities, or privileges of family, of birth, or country?

Why withhold a kindness when it costs you nothing?
What cost is a smile?

Embrace what you do not have,
and you will have all that you need.

CHAPTER 7: EXAMINING OUR PATH

Walk where no one else has gone,
yet many wish they had.

Path Rules

You are on a path. Once you take a step, you cannot go back to where you were. Each moment you can choose to follow a new path. Sometimes you must wait for the new path to appear. Changing from a bigger path to a smaller path often takes time. Everyone must walk on big paths from time to time. You can walk in circles, but even then the path is still different. The path always forms before you and leaves a trace behind you.

"The Path" is a metaphor for our choices and decisions in our life-journey. There is no shame in finding out that the path you were on was not the one you were meant to walk.

Ultimately a man travels his chosen path alone.
Shared paths bring joy.

What is your path like? *(Create your own koan.)*

_____

_____

Mission to Many, Journey of One

Your mission statement is what you do. It clarifies your goals and how you are going to accomplish them. What is your process of life discovery? *(Create your own koan.)*

_____

_____

Complete your journey to find your way to the great path.

Motivation

Are you internally or externally motivated? We all need a bit of a kick-start from time to time, but where does the energy come from to persevere?

A spark lights a flame,
but a candle only burns as long as the wick.

Live with cause. Leave the results to be determined.

When are you inspired? When do you inspire others? *(Create your own koan.)*

_____

_____

Motivation gets you started; habit keeps you going.

Many roads lead to the great path;
only the willing find their way.

What are your Dreams?

It is quite common for adults to ask children and teens, *"What they want to be or to do when they grow up?"* Yet, many adults themselves are unsatisfied with their lives, but stop dreaming about achieving anything better than their current circumstances. Why? Imagine that all possible obstacles were pushed aside; is there anything that you would still like to accomplish?

"May your successes, exceed your wildest dreams."
Marianne Schneider Corey

In a perfect world, what would you still like to accomplish? *(Create your own koan.)*

_____

_____

What steps do you need to take?

Theoretically, Spiritual Zen encompasses the whole universe, yet unfolds with the most insignificant action. ***What matters most is not what life throws at us, but how we respond to it.***
The question is not what is the meaning of life? Rather, how can I respond to life meaningfully?

> ***"Routines are good medicine."*** Silvia Gonzalez-Baeza

What type of plan, motivation, and routines do you need? *(Create your own koan.)*

Who are you?

How would you describe yourself? *(values, beliefs, attitudes)*

Did you describe your character or personality? Our personality is often what we show to others based upon how we feel about ourselves—our self-esteem. Our character tends to be based on our deeper beliefs and values—our self-worth.

Character

What is it that defines our character? The psychiatrist Frank Pittman stated:

> *"The stability of our lives depends upon our character. It is character, not passion that keeps marriages together long enough to do their work of raising children into mature, responsible, productive citizens. In this imperfect world it is character that enables people to survive, to endure, and to transcend their misfortunes."*

In her book **BUILDING MORAL INTELLIGENCE** author Michelle Borba identified seven essential virtues that form a persons character:

empathy, conscience, self-control, respect, kindness, tolerance and fairness. Which of these qualities would you like to work on? What is in your way of being able to demonstrate your best character in all situations?

A person's true nature is decided in the struggle between conscious intention and subconscious desires.
Unity happens when flow conquers ego.

Are we who we choose to be? *(Create your own koan.)*

_____

_____

From Dependent to Interdependent

We all start life totally dependent on the safety of our Mother's womb. After our birth we remain dependent on our parents or caregivers for many years. It is a common misconception that as we mature, we should strive to be fully independent. However, as human beings, we need each other in many different ways. Forming meaningful and lasting relationships with others is never an easy task. We all know that relationships have both risks and rewards but what is the alternative? Loneliness was the first thing in the Christian Bible that God said was not good.

Risking yourself,
is being open to experiencing more than your self.

What does it mean to you to be interdependent with others? *(Create your own koan.)*

_____

_____

Creating Healthy Relationships

Today's world is dominated by electronically mediated means of communicating with each other. How connected you are to social media or the right social media has become a measuring rod of effective communication.

Yet, it seems like many of the basic skills of interacting with each other in face-to-face interactions have fallen into disuse and that simple social graces—manners—have gotten lost in the electronic buzz.

Is there a way to use our understanding of Spiritual Zen practice to improve our daily interactions with others? Let's start by looking at suggestions for interacting with strangers and build towards our relationships with those closest to us. Have you ever passed an unhappy person on the street or saw someone who was upset on a bus or in a waiting room? What would it cost you to offer a kind word of encouragement or a warm and supportive smile?

It is often the gift from a stranger that has the biggest impact, as there is no reason for them to act in a kind manner except out of their own goodness.

What gift can you offer a stranger that becomes a gift to yourself? *(Create your own koan.)*

_____

_____

When was the last time you took a few minutes to get to know someone better who otherwise was only an acquaintance to you? What if you made it a goal to find at least one thing you had in common with that other person.

What are the qualities most lacking in relationships in the work environment?

The way to succeed is to help others succeed. *(Create your own koan.)*

_____

_____

How much time do you spend each day, week or month, in person with friends and family? Quality time is important, but if there is an insufficient quantity of time together, the quality of time together will be more wishful thinking than reality. If you have a partner or spouse, how would you characterize the style of communication you have with each other?

When was the last time when you felt that you really connected with that person on several different levels at the same time *(mentally, emotionally, physically, spiritually)*?

What is a soul mate, if not a person to share the journey of life with?

(Create your own koan.)

_____

_____

Family Spirit

Part of establishing a healthy family structure is setting the boundaries that keep family members safe but allow each person to grow and become their own person.

What is your family's theme or mantra? *(Create your own koan.)*

_____

_____

Family Rule: We meet each other's needs, not always each other's wants.

Happiness and Fulfillment

Do you believe that your natural state is one of peace and contentment? A Spiritual Zen perspective believes that the core of our spirit is inner purity and goodness.

The secret to happiness is low expectations, but high aspirations.

What is your secret to happiness? *(Create your own koan.)*

_____

_____

CHAPTER 8: BLOCKS TO SPIRITUAL FLOW

Struggling with Addictions

No one starts out deciding that they want to become an addict when they grow up. Addictions develop from negative life experiences, poor choices, and exposure to addictive substances. A person's reasons for acting out tend to fall into one of there categories: **approach** *(they desire the experience)*, **avoidance** *(they wish to avoid or escape mental, emotional or physical pain)*, or **against** *(they are trying to send a message to others by hurting themselves)*. When we experience anything in life such as pain, we can respond by moving towards, away, or against.

For example we can move **towards ourselves** *(self-help, introspection)*, **towards others** *(reaching out and talking to someone else)*, or **towards source** *(prayer, meditation)*. Similarly we can **avoid ourselves** *(escapist behaviors, alter our reality with chemicals)*, **avoid others** *(isolation, disengaging from close relationships)* or **avoid source** *(refusing to acknowledge our spiritual nature or connection)*. Lastly, we can move **against ourselves** *(self-abuse, self-harm, self-deprecation)*, **against others** *(blaming others, getting angry at others, harming others)*, or **against source** *(blaming source [God], taking our anger out on religious persons and so forth)*. At all times we are making a conscious or unconscious choice. Even not acting—sleeping as much as possible is still a choice.

Almost any behavior can become addictive in nature. Common behavioral addictions include: compulsive shopping, gambling, sexual disinhibitions, and the use of food to mediate emotions. Addictions to substances such as alcohol and drugs create a very real physical dependency and often require medically supervised withdrawal.

Consider ten people who break their leg and get temporarily put on morphine for the pain. Nine out of ten people are easily able to reduce the use of the morphine as their pain subsides.

However, the tenth person develops a craving for the morphine and desires more even after their physical pain has lessened. What is going on with that person? The simple explanation is that the morphine on some level was perceived by the person to lessen their pre-existing mental and emotional pain. The morphine then became a *"solution"* to more than physical pain.

Addiction is compulsively seeking solutions outside of yourself. *Deiderik Wolsak*

From a Spiritual Zen perspective an addiction develops when a person's natural flow of energy is blocked by a perceived need that sucks in energy but gives nothing back. The suffering person is trying to feel better by acting out in a manner that might give temporary relief but offers no long-term solution. It is like trying to water a tree at the end of the yard with a long hose that is full of holes. The water goes into the hose but never gets to the tree.

Recovery is often a slow process that incorporates a change in thinking, emotional responses, and new behaviors. The key to recovery is in creating a new relationship with yourself, with others and trusting that the *universe* only wants what is in your best interest.

Freedom from suffering is as easy as focusing your attention away from yourself.

Act out Love not Pain

Are you are acting-out mental, physical or emotional pain through some form of self-abuse such as: over-eating, substance abuse, or risky behaviors? Who are you trying to punish and why? Hurting yourself to send a message to someone else is only hurting you.

Match the intensity of the hurt-pain with love, until the past dissolves away.

Sometimes it takes the interaction with another caring person who can verbally acknowledge and validate the your past painful experience allowing it to be labeled or *"anchored,"* so that it can be released. Therapeutically working through the anchors dissolves the stale energy and allows our spiritual energy to flow freely once again.

Why do you complain about what you do not have?
Look within and discover nothing.
Yet everything needed is there.

People heal mentally and emotionally at their own rate. As the therapist is healing and pealing off the protective layers as they appear in surface behaviors, the person is at the same time growing their inner core spirit and personal resiliency so that they do not need so many protective layers.

"The human sees suffering.
The soul sees love." Linda Rose

Depending on the intensity of our past hurts, our psychic pain may need to be validated again and again, until we can let it go. For some, it is like letting air get at the wound, so that it can heal naturally. For others it is exploring all aspects of the past injury with a caring therapist, so that it can be understood.

Then the event or events can be put in their proper context, such as: *"You were a child then, and had no control over the situation. You are an adult now, and can choose to respond differently."*

One of the hardest challenges in life,
is to learn how to stand up for yourself - appropriately.

Once a dysfunctional coping behavior is repeated
it becomes self-reinforcing.

Displaced in Time

For many people the root of their suffering is a perspective of time. Dwelling on the past is a trap and leads to depression. Overly focusing on an uncertain future leads to anxiety.

What is the past and future? Eternity is always now.

Are you living under Oppression?

Life is to be lived as a bird flies, or as a fish swims in the water. If you are suffering under the tyranny of circumstances you are not able to fulfill your potential. If you are oppressed or constrained in any way *(emotionally, socially, financially)* you have lost some of your freedom.

Sometimes our own choices and actions place us in difficult circumstances and sometimes it is other people imposing their power by fraud or force over us.

Freedom is exercising self-ownership over your time, talents, and resources. We have one life. Live it!

The goal as we grow up is not to become fully independent, but interdependent with others in a healthy way. Unhealthy relationships may happen when people become overly dependent on each other. They use their energy to influence the other person to get their needs met and sometimes this is mutual; sometimes it is unidirectional.

What cannot be bought or sold; yet everyone must have?

You stole everything else, but left my heart. I still have all I need.

Relationships with people who are overly independent tend to result in a competition for each other's time, talent, and treasure. Love may be withheld or conditionally given out, and resources may be selfishly hoarded.

The important point is that we choose or allow these types of relationships to develop and we can choose to change them or walk away.

Apologies take Courage

Sometimes, if we are to make a healthy change in our lives, we need to make a sincere apology to another person or several people to be able to move forward. Remember that a good apology has four parts: I am sorry, it was my fault, it will not happen again, and what can I do to make things better?

Allowing Grief to Flow

Everyone processes their thoughts, feelings, and past experiences in different ways. If your feelings of grief are interfering with your daily functioning—then it is time to acknowledge those feelings and anchor the energy. The identified grief issue may now be worked through and in the process you release the blockage and allow your spirit to flow.

When your spiritual energy flows freely you will release the stale energy and return to a dynamic energy equilibrium.

Is fear holding you back?

From a Spiritual Zen perspective fear blocks the free flow of spiritual energy. It is hanging onto the negative energy associated with what might happen, allowing the fear to control us. If we accept each situation as if we had chosen it, then the question becomes: *"What shall I do now?"*

Letting go of fear is non-attachment to emotions. It is allowing yourself to acknowledge the fear but rechannel your energy in a positive direction. For some people it might be a sorting out process. Is this something within my control or outside of my control? For other people it is recognizing that fear is your ego—the illusion of yourself being unduly influenced by others or wanting to influence or control situations or people in a manner that interferes with their free will.

> *My spirit is eternal. I have nothing to fear.*
> *The peace of the universe is within me.*

CHAPTER 9: FACILITATING SPIRITUAL FLOW

Start with Acceptance

What are you feeling right now? How is your energy level? Is there anything that you are unhappy about in any area of your life? *(Spiritual, Mental, Emotional, Social or Physical)* If so, take a moment to just accept your situation—just as it is.

> *When we accept our circumstances,*
> *we find peace.*
> *When we embrace our ability to choose,*
> *we find power.*
> *When peace and power are in balance, we find joy!*

Very few of us are totally happy with our lives. Most of us would like to make changes, little changes, big changes, or perhaps changing our whole life direction. Each of us guards the gate of change that can only be opened from the inside. Even if you are ready, where do you start? How can you change if you do not know who you are?

> *You cannot reach enlightenment*
> *if you do not believe that you are worthy.*

Taking back the Power

A person's actions usually flow from their values, beliefs and attitudes. Values tend to be quite deeply rooted, beliefs are more malleable and attitudes are the most fluid. Looking at where behaviors originate and what they are based upon provides a starting point for change.

The Spiritual Zen process of change begins with our thinking—a firm resolution to do something new! The direction of flow is: **Think** *(head)*, **Feel** *(heart)*, **Act** *(hands)*. Some people tend to be led by their emotions but what happens when you do not feel like doing what you know you need to do.

Other people may not know what they should do, or be afraid to take chances and seem to float through life like they are on a purposeless treadmill.

Changing your Path

No one can take your chosen path away from you. Only you can choose to walk in a different direction. While our paradigm may change in an instant, making lasting changes to our life often takes determination, resources and time.

To whom much is given—much is expected!

Whole-Hearted Living

Healthy people remain flexible, regardless of the situation, with robust values at their core. Therefore, getting to know you and affirming your core values is a great first step. Having a strong core helps us to withstand the storms of circumstances as well as appreciate the beautiful sunny days.

Giving out of your abundance is great. What if you are the type of person who tends to give more than you typically receive? Realize that it is important to take care of yourself—so that you may take care of others.

Give according to your ability;
take according to your need.

Flowing Love into Challenging Relationships *(personal freedom)*

People who take advantage of others often have what is described as a low level of emotional maturity. This may be a short-term period, while they were going through a particularly rough time in their own life or a longer-term pattern of behavior and manner of acting towards others.

In business, people with low levels of emotional maturity tend to *"borrow strength"* from positional authority, credentials, past achievements, and status symbols. The outcome is almost always damaging to the employer/employee relationship, which often leaves the employee feeling resentful.

Love leads. Love flows. Love fills.

People with low levels of emotional maturity tend to be overly moody, seek to control or overtly influence the actions of others. They may constantly have high expectations of others and then blame profusely when disappointed. The point is that they do not have the other person's best interests in mind.

People with high levels of emotional maturity, seem to be more sensitive to how the other person is doing and what the other person's real needs are. They demonstrate emotional: flexibility, honesty, openness, the ability to see alternative points of view, and are nonjudgmental.

Shared pain is a joy.
Hidden pain blocks flow.
Release your pain and fly.

Affirming Abundance

Spiritual Zen is not just reaching out to and connecting with others. You need to have a great relationship with yourself first. Learning to affirm your positive intentions is a practice that can become a habit. A good affirmation is personal, positive, and present tense. It is visual, tangible, and emotional. Consider the example below. Can you create your own meaningful affirmations?

I am a child of the universe,
forever loved, beautiful both inside and out.
I am both worthy of love and capable of loving others.

Discovering your own Metaphor for Life

Zen is a path that unfolds with each step. Spiritual Zen is opening oneself up to the waves of source vibrations that continue to wash over us. Choosing a wave to surf is trusting in the ocean of energy to carry you on. What metaphor best describes your life-journey? *(walk-path, swim-water, fly-air)*

You can never move forward
if you are always looking back.

You must release your burden,
before you can find your own way.

Improving Your Meditative Practice – Flow Meditation

Would you like to improve your meditative practice, but do not know where to start? The following are some suggestions that might be helpful:

- If at all possible find a place where you can regularly practice *"quiet listening,"* but remember that you carry your *"bubble of peace"* with you where ever you go. Even in a busy shopping mall, you can stop and take a moment in your head to reconnect with your spirit.

- Decide right now that you want mindfulness *(prayer, meditation)* to be a part of your life, practiced daily at pre-determined times and throughout your day. The simplest prayer is one of gratitude and appreciation *"Thank You (source) for ...!"*

- When you look at yourself in the mirror, do you see love looking back at you? If not, try creating some positive affirmations that you can repeat until you see yourself as worthy of love and able to freely receive and give love.

- Are you relationships with others characterized by co-operation, conflict or competition? Try in your meditations to project positive healthy energy into those relationships. Imagine real natural physical results flowing from your spiritual intentions of peace and harmony.

- Strive to see yourself as an energy conduit, receiving all you need from the universe and flowing out abundant energy to others. Keep your vertical *(universe)* connection open, to be able to give horizontally to others. Keep giving to keep receiving. When we stop giving freely to others, we lose our connection to the universal flow of spiritual energy.

- Do you see yourself as a drop of water in the ocean, tossed and blown about or as a vital part of the ecology of life on earth? Try to envision yourself as part of a vast system of spiritual energy—spiritually connected to others and flowing with source energy to accomplish your specific role in a shared collective purpose.

- How much of your time is focused on acquiring things rather than spending quality time with people that you care about?

- Is there a way that you can have all that you need *(not want)* and still enjoy a fulfilled life?

- Do you see your life as an opportunity for personal transformation and a time of preparation for spiritual transcendence? What can you do in the *"here and now"* to raise your spiritual vibration to better connect with source energy?

- Can you create your own koans that speak to the deeper core truths of your own life so that when the meaning is understood the words become unnecessary?

- Lastly, what is your special gift that you can share freely with others at no cost to yourself?

Spiritual Zen is transformation to enlightenment through dynamically experiencing your own connection to the universe.

When I am OK with me, I can connect with you.

EPILOGUE

Did you see the flowers of Spiritual Zen as you walked through the pages of this book? If you did, I hope that you only glimpsed them, appreciated their beauty, and walked on.

Everybody possesses the great truth of Spiritual Zen.

*Look deeply into your own being and
see others looking back at you.*

My personal truth is that as humans we were created for the purpose of forming relationships. The fullness of life is experienced through discovering, embracing and letting go of both the joy and pain of these relationships. Our physical existence is transitory. It is our spiritual essence that is eternal and a part of the spiritual flow of the universe.

Whether you choose to experience a deep relationship with yourself, with others and with a universal spiritual vibration that is up to you. Your personal truth is intricately interwoven with your journey in life.

Silence

Funny how we often go for a walk, when we want to find *source*. Somewhere in the forest, maybe near a quiet babbling brook. Yes, *source* is there, or perhaps on a mountaintop with a spectacular view. It seems that *source* does not usually stand out in our every day lives unless something out of the ordinary happens.

Today, I saw *source* in everything, all my surroundings, the people around me, and life. *Source* is not some mythical being way up there, *source* is in us, the birds, the trees and the wind in our hair. *Source* is present downtown on a busy street amid all the noise and bustle. *Source* is not present only in silence, so when we are silent, it's nice to take the time to thank *source* for all the rest of the time. For life is *source;* and living is beautiful with *source.*

Show me how to be grateful for this day, for the people around me, my life, my community, for the world in which we live. Give me the strength to grow, to love, to live; and *Source* if I get a moment of silence, let me thank you.

It is through losing someone who you love dearly,
that you are able to learn to love others better.

"It is hard to live your own life if it is defined by another's
wisdom." (BKB)

If I did not have the mountain to walk around,
I would have missed much of my journey.

© Doug Pamenter 26 May 2015

www.ingramcontent.com/pod-product-compliance
Lightning Source LLC
Chambersburg PA
CBHW071024040426
42443CB00007B/929